THE ART OF RESELLING SNEAKERS:

How To Make Money Reselling Sneakers Like A Pro

Presented By CloseoutExplosion.com

By
Donny Lowy

Copyright © 2023
All Rights Reserved
Donny Lowy

Table of Contents

How to Resell Sneakers As a Reseller _____ 1

Where to Buy Wholesale Sneakers _____ 3

How to Buy Sneakers in Bulk _____ 5

How to Buy Wholesale Sneakers From Alibaba _____ 7

How to Buy Sneakers From DHgate _____ 9

Can You Resell Shoes Online? _____ 11

How Much Does It Cost To Start Reselling Sneakers? _____ 13

Is Buying and Selling Sneakers Worth It? _____ 15

Where Can I Sell My Sneakers For the Most Money? _____ 17

Selling Sneakers on Poshmark _____ 19

Selling Sneakers on ThredUP and Poshmark _____ 21

Selling Sneakers on The RealReal _____ 23

Selling Sneakers on Flyp _____ 25

How to Make Money Selling Shoes Online _____ 27

Tips For Buying on the Kixify Marketplace _____ 29

How to Sell Sneakers to Grailed _____ 31

Selling Sneakers and Streetwear on StockX _____ 33

Selling Sneakers on Heroine _____ 36

Selling Sneakers on Tradesy _____ 38

Unmasking the Authenticity: A Comprehensive Guide to Sneaker Authentication and Counterfeit Detection _____ 41

Sneaker Release Strategies and the Phenomenon of Drop Culture: An In-depth Analysis _____ 44

Sneaker Collaborations and Limited Editions: A Revolution in Footwear Culture _____ 47

Sneaker Cleaning and Restoration Techniques _____ 50

60 Super Popular And Hot Sneaker Brands For Resellers _____ 54

10 Sneaker Trade Shows That Sneaker Resellers Will Love _____ 60

Ready To Manufacture Your Own Sneaker Line? These 10 Sneaker Factories Are Ready To Make Your Dreams Come True! _____ 62

Conclusion: _____ 64

How to Resell Sneakers As a Reseller

As a new reseller, you may be wondering: How to resell sneakers? There are some tips you should follow to make your sneakers more valuable. You should aim buy products at below wholesale or closeout prices, as the market for sneaker reselling is highly competitive, but price alone should never be the determining factor. However, you should make sure that you choose products that have long-term value. For example, you may want to buy new sneakers on release day, when they are still available for retail prices. Another option is to join consignment stores, which act as middlemen between buyers and sellers. Alternatively, you can try direct transactions through sites like StockX by Josh Luber.

Another tip to resell your sneakers is to research the price of the sneakers you want to sell. Check out the average price of similar sneakers in your area, as well as their trend over the past 12 months. Then, decide how much to charge for each pair. If you're new to the market, it may take time to gain trust from buyers, but don't give up. Start by looking for pairs that have sold for under reseller prices.

Secondly, you should check the comments left by previous buyers before purchasing. Some people might have complaints about the delivery time or the quality of the sneakers, but you should make sure that these are genuine reviews. Some people may write fake reviews just to boost their seller's rating, while others may post fake reviews. In any case, you should trust your instincts. You can easily spot fake reviews online. You can also search local Facebook groups for updates on hype.

Lastly, if you are serious about growing your resale business, it is important to know the target audience. A good customer retention rate can lead to a steady stream of new sales. In the sneaker industry, this strategy is considered one of the most effective methods. In other words, your customers will likely buy more from you if they know you already. You should consider retaining customers to build a strong brand name.

Buying and selling shoes for resale is similar to trading stocks - some shoes are hot and some don't. Some sneakers get a lot of attention and sell fast, but then fade out over time. To find the right shoe to invest in, you should read the Hypemaster Playbook. You should also read reviews to determine whether a certain shoe will sell well and make you money. It's not as hard as it seems - just follow the tips below to get started selling sneakers and make some extra cash.

Using a CRM software will help you track your interactions with clients and potential customers. This will also help you save time. In addition to CRM software, you should conduct market research and find out how much customers are buying sneakers. Some sneaker resellers even hire market research firms to do the research for them. Aside from this, you'll also need design tools such as Adobe Photoshop and Illustrator. These design programs will cost you $10-50 per month.

Where to Buy Wholesale Sneakers

With so many footwear wholesalers in the sneaker market, it can be difficult to choose a good supplier. Finding the right one is crucial for a successful store, and this chapter will guide you to the top wholesale suppliers. Start shopping for wholesale sneakers today! There are some easy steps to take before buying wholesale sneakers. Using an online wholesale directory can help you get started! Read on for some tips and tricks! Below are three great places to look for wholesale sneakers.

Footsites - The best places to buy wholesale sneakers are sites run by the same company but function independently. For example, you can buy Air Jordan 1s on Footaction, Champs Sport, and Eastbay, but you will need to use different payment information for each pair. These sites also have different sizing policies, so don't forget to check the GS size first! Buying a pair of sneakers from an individual is an excellent way to ensure authenticity. Usually, retail stores have a one pair per customer policy.

When buying wholesale sneakers, keep in mind that the market changes often. You need to keep your finger on the pulse of what is popular and what isn't. While it may seem hard to know which products are hot and which ones aren't, you can use the SaleHoo Labs feature to find what's selling well. While a large variety is great, there are also certain types of sneakers that will make more profit for you.

Marmedia - A German company called Marmedia has an extensive list of wholesale sneakers from top sports brands. Marmedia offers over 90 brands. They supply wholesale sneakers to boutiques, eCommerce sites, and luxury retailers. It is a great place to source wholesale sneakers. You can even pre-order the new collections for the coming season if you don't want to miss them. It's worth checking out if you're looking to start a new business.

Find a supplier with a minimum order requirement. Buying a sample of the shoe is a great way to make sure that you're getting a good fit, or even a size that you can afford to trade for. Remember, it's better to get a small quantity and build your inventory slowly. Selling shoes is not an easy business, so make sure to research your suppliers carefully. You'll also want to know what type of payment methods they offer.

Consider local shoe stores. They'll often have overstock items that you can buy at a discount. These shoes aren't necessarily the latest style, but they'll do for your business demographic. Another option is to check with the manufacturer directly. This way, you'll be sure that the quality is good, and you can resell them at a high price. And don't forget to check the seasonality of the shoes.

Look for a retailer that offers a free trial period. Some resellers sell shoes by the pallet, which is also known as a lot. Since you can't choose what's inside a pallet, it's best to research the seller carefully. You'll have a chance to find a good deal by purchasing a single pair. When purchasing shoes, it's better to compare prices than pay full price.

How to Buy Sneakers in Bulk

There are a few different ways to buy sneakers in bulk, and if you're looking for the easiest way to get a large amount of kicks at a discounted price, here are a few suggestions:

Before buying in bulk, be aware of the cancellation risks. While you can usually buy several pairs with one credit card, it's not guaranteed. Another option is to join a cooking group and ask more experienced people for advice on the subject. That way, you can get the best possible deals without the risk of wasting money. The best way to buy in bulk is to find a vendor who will help you buy in bulk.

One of the biggest challenges in building a successful resale business is securing limited-edition sneakers. To do this, you'll need to buy bots or join "cook" groups where other buyers and consignors share information and resources. This is an expensive and time-consuming process, which adds to the high barrier to entry for the sneaker resale industry.

Once you know how many pairs you'd like to order, you can contact the supplier and make an offer. Make sure you have room to store the shoes and packaging materials to ship them to your customers. Ask for samples of the products you want to purchase and check the quality. If the MOQ is too high, try to negotiate a smaller order size with the supplier. Be sure to use a secure payment method, as this will eliminate the risk of fraud. If you're not able to do this, find another supplier that will.

If you want to save money on shipping and packaging costs, you should consider importing the sneakers directly from China. If you don't want to spend money on shipping, consider selling them online. Some retailers allow you to sell wholesale sneakers directly. These websites offer a large selection of products at low prices. And you can save a significant amount of money when you buy sneakers in bulk. This way, you can save money while buying shoes that are in demand.

When buying sneakers online, you can use a service that

sources products from leading manufacturers in China. They have over 46,000 sneakers in their warehouse, and their website is user-friendly and easy to navigate. They also offer a dispute center. If you're unsure of how to choose the right sneakers for your business, try Global Sources. If you're new to online purchasing, you can use Made-in-China.

Try to find a wholesale supplier of sneakers in the United States. Some dropship directories allow you to search for suppliers in your state. Some even have international shipping, so you can ship anywhere! Also, if you have a website, you can also search for these wholesalers. If you're looking for a reputable supplier, Spocket is a great place to start your search. They're not far from your doorstep and will ship the sneakers right to your customers.

How to Buy Wholesale Sneakers From Alibaba

If you want to buy wholesale sneakers from Alibaba., you can find out about the procedures from the information provided in this article. However, it is vital to be very confident in your negotiation skills and make sure you do not leave the negotiations in the middle of the process. This can be hard to do as some online marketers focus on attracting clients and sell fake items. However, it is possible to spot these fakes by following these simple tips.

First, sign up for an account in Alibaba.com. You do not need to have a wholesaler license in order to register with Alibaba.com. Once you do, go to the "Shoes & Accessories" tab and choose the style and color of shoes you want. Select a few suppliers and compare their prices to get the best deal. This will show your supplier that you know what you want and you have the confidence to bargain. If the supplier wants your business, they will be happy to offer you the best deal possible.

When looking for shoes, you should look for manufacturers who offer high-quality sneakers. Make sure that the manufacturer's website features facts about its products. This will help you narrow down which brands are best-selling and which ones aren't. Also, check out reviews from existing customers so you can decide which ones you want to purchase. This way, you'll have a better idea of which brands are worth investing in.

While it is possible to find many suppliers in Alibaba, you have to know which ones are legitimate. Most of the Alibaba suppliers are manufacturers. Those who offer low prices will often sell to liquidators and wholesalers, because they can afford to buy in bulk and store large amounts of inventory. But most retailers will not be able to contact these suppliers directly. You may find a small manufacturer who will work directly with you.

The best way to buy wholesale sneakers for resale is by cutting deals with the designer yourself. Since you're buying wholesale shoes from a manufacturer, you'll get good deals, and they are more likely to sell for a decent profit. Plus, this way, you won't have to take the risk of buying from foreign manufacturers who are not known for quality control. In addition, the shoes will be in higher demand if they are timeless.

Once you've found a supplier, you can ask for quotations and information. Alibaba has a verification system, which alerts buyers to the historical accuracy of each manufacturer. Make sure you communicate with the supplier through an official representative. The payment method of your choice should be secure, as long as it allows you to avoid scams. Also, keep in mind that you might encounter fake sellers if you don't know how to use it.

How to Buy Sneakers From DHgate

There are many ways to buy sneakers from DHgate. However, you must be aware of some important things to ensure the authenticity of your purchase. First, you need to read the seller's feedback to ensure their honesty and trustworthiness. Some sellers might use Photoshop to cover up any deformities. To avoid these, you can look at the actual product pictures. Some sellers might even post a masked image of their sneakers. To avoid falling prey to this scam, you should try to get a genuine image of the sneakers by messaging them.

If you're interested in buying sneakers on a budget, you can use the DHGate marketplace to buy them at a discounted price. This site is also the second largest marketplace in the world, which makes it difficult to find a good seller. While DHGate offers the lowest prices, you must be careful when buying from the Chinese marketplace as many sellers are shady. Ensure that the seller you're dealing with has a positive rating in order to avoid fraud.

Dhgate is a huge marketplace, but a few sellers are notorious for selling fake shoes. Even if you're looking to purchase replicas, it is important to keep these in mind. In general, these are cheap replicas. On StockX, however, you can expect to pay a little more, but authentic shoes won't be available at that price. A good way to make sure you get a quality product at a good price is to sign up for a newsletter that lets you know when prices go up.

While you can buy replica sneakers on other sites, you need to be aware that these shoes are not as durable as the originals. They will wear out in months or even years. This is especially true if you're going to spend $50 on a pair of sneakers. Even though the price of these sneakers might be low compared to a $15 pair from Wish, you'll still need to be sure of their quality. However, you should avoid buying replica sneakers from standalone websites and Instagram stores.

One of the best-known DHGate sellers is Boost700V2 store. This store sells a variety of shoes ranging from Nike and Adidas to casual sneakers. It has more than 30,000 satisfied customers and a 99.3% positive feedback. It also sells replica designer canvas shoes. The shoes are well-made and look great on the feet. The prices here are very reasonable. If you're looking for a replica shoe, this is the best place to start.

DHgate also offers a variety of shoes. You can find the most popular types of sneakers by browsing the overall transactions of the site. You can also see the materials used to make these sneakers. You can also check out the Men Designer Shoes store, which has both high-quality replicas and affordable price ranges. There's even a store for suede sneakers, so you don't have to worry about wearing a fake. Besides, you can always throw them out after wearing them for a couple of times and replace them for a cheaper price.

Can You Resell Shoes Online?

There are many ways to resell sneakers. Some resellers use real estate in their homes to store shoes, which saves money but takes up space. There are also many hidden costs, including bots, backdooring rates, cook groups, seller fees, shipping expenses, and more. If you decide to resell shoes online, be sure to invest some money. You might not even be able to break even if you don't have a lot of cash.

Although it is not illegal to resell purchased items, it's important to remember that some manufacturers have little control of their products after they've been sold. Even if you're not selling counterfeit products, you can still get them for a lower price than the original retail price. You could also try painting them yourself - a great idea! And of course, reselling them is the best way to support the local economy.

Although sneaker reselling is a lucrative endeavor, you still have to pay taxes on the money you make. For high-volume resellers, you'll be considered a self-employed business, but for low-volume sellers, you can declare your profits as hobby income. Keep in mind that pending tax laws may allow the IRS to track all bank transactions and require all parties to report interactions. As a result, if you sell sneakers for more than retail, the reseller price is a valid tax deduction. And remember to include the cost of shipping and sales tax.

Reselling shoes online is similar to trading stocks. Some shoes go viral in the beginning, but then fade in popularity. In order to avoid this, you'll need to get a retail store and a legitimate business license. The best way to sell sneakers online is to sell them for less than retail prices. However, you must be honest in your descriptions. It may take a while to earn the trust of buyers, but keep marching forward.

Sneaker reselling can be lucrative, but beware! There are some pitfalls to keep in mind. First, you need to understand the market. If you're selling to a random person, you might find that he's not as honest as you thought. Don't forget to keep your contact information confidential. Beware of the people claiming to be your buyers. They may be disgruntled with the way you sell sneakers.

Another way to resell shoes online is through a consignment store. A consignment store serves as a middleman between the seller and buyer. Conversely, you can sell to a sneakerhead directly through a website. Other reselling methods involve Facebook groups, Craigslist, and eBay. For more information, visit StockX by Josh Luber. You'll find thousands of shoes for sale online.

Another option is selling your old sneakers via stadium goods. Stadium Goods allows you to list your sneakers on their consignment website and ship them directly to them. If you sell your shoes via stadium goods, they will handle the sale on your behalf and earn 80 percent of the list price. You will receive payment through direct deposit in three to five business days. You may also receive payment directly through your bank account. If you're a small-time reselling business, you may get away without any legal issues.

How Much Does It Cost To Start Reselling Sneakers?

How much does it cost to start resaling sneakers? You may be thinking: "How much does it cost to start reselling sneakers?" It all depends on what you want to sell. A great place to start is eBay. Depending on your budget, you can sell your own sneakers or buy them from an online broker. Regardless of which route you choose, you will need at least $150,000 to get started.

There are many ways to get started, from online stores to brick & mortar locations. You may need to invest in equipment such as a washing machine, air compressor, and shelving. Marketing your shoes may be more involved, with social media contests and raffles. However, the initial costs may be low compared to the expenses of operating your business. And since you'll be competing with experts in the field, a mentor will accelerate your learning curve and save you money in the long run.

The most important element of reselling sneakers is an eye for limited releases. Many big trainer companies release a limited number of new sneakers each year, and collectors line up at the sneaker stores to get their hands on them. Some people blag these sneakers to wear, and then sell them immediately afterwards, but the shoes will be in mint condition. In addition to being in mint condition, they'll also increase in value exponentially.

Another important factor in starting a reselling business is a budget. There are many ways to buy and sell sneakers, and some people use real estate in their home. Using real estate in your home for storage is an option, but it does require a substantial amount of space. Additionally, there are many hidden costs in shoe reselling. There are bots, backdooring rates, cook groups, seller fees, and shipping and travel expenses to name a few. So before you start reselling sneakers, you need to determine what your budget is.

Another important element is the pricing of the sneakers. Some high-end sneakers, like Jordan 1 Highs, go for $200 to $200, and are regularly selling over $300 on the aftermarket. While these prices are not necessarily the highest you can charge for sneakers, they'll certainly bring you money. If you're selling cheaply, you'll probably have trouble finding buyers. To find a price range that matches your inventory, look for apps like SNKRS and Nike's Goat. These apps are safer than other platforms, since the sellers are asked to provide more information.

Another option is to try eBay. eBay has become the oldest online venue for reselling sneakers. eBay recently rebranded its stake in the footwear market. Authenticity guarantees are required, and you will have to pay the cost of shipping to the authentication partner. Whether you're selling a new or used pair, eBay will charge a flat fee of up to 9.5 percent of the total transaction value. If you're selling a second-hand pair of sneakers, Flight Club charges a $5 fee. Finally, it also requires a cashout fee of 2.9 percent.

Is Buying and Selling Sneakers Worth It?

Is buying and reselling sneakers worth it? It can be a lucrative business, but there are risks. Sneaker reselling is a time-consuming process, and it can also lead to scams. While some people have made their money through this venture, others have been taken advantage of. Here are some tips to help you avoid buying a fake pair of sneakers. Although there are a few ways to spot a scam, they should not be used as the sole method.

First, find the popular brands of sneakers. This will make it easier to spot fakes and research pricing. Adidas and Nike are both trusted sneaker brands. Research what colorways and silhouettes sell the best to get the best price. If possible, try using bots to automate your search. Using bots to do your research is also an option, but it is still recommended to be thorough. In some cases, you can find the best-selling shoes by checking Facebook groups in your locality.

Another tip for finding a good pair is to keep your eyes open for limited editions. Sneakers from high-end brands tend to sell better than others. Sneaker Don, for example, drives the price of Travis Scotts and other high-end sneakers. This is because these sneakers will be hard to find, and you can often find them cheaper online than at retail. Conversely, mejia sells low-quality Air Maxes and Air Forces.

To sell your sneaker online, you should keep in mind the rules of each site. Most sites offer a fee structure, but it is worthwhile to look at the history of popular sneakers on the market before listing them. This can help you determine if the price is too high or too low. If you're not sure, you can use a site called StockX to see what others have paid for the same sneakers.

Selling sneakers is a lucrative business. If you know how to market yourself, you can make a six-figure income. You can start as a side hustle or as a full-time business. Just make sure that you invest your time and effort into reselling sneakers. Remember that success is not overnight, so make sure you're ready to put in the work. You will be glad you did.

The culture of sneaker reselling isn't without its challenges. One of the biggest challenges is the high cost of the product. The demand for the product is higher than the supply. Buying from a reseller can make the shoes you're selling more than double what you paid for them. And you'll be surprised at how much money you can get if you know how to handle the hassles.

Reselling sneakers on StockX isn't an easy business, and you'll need patience to make money. There's no get-rich-quick scheme here, and if you don't have patience, it won't work out. It is also important to understand that this business is not for the faint of heart, as you'll likely end up frustrated if you don't get your money fast.

Where Can I Sell My Sneakers For the Most Money?

If you have a pair of sneakers, you may be wondering where to sell them for the most money. The answer depends on your location and what you're selling. Online marketplaces, such as eBay and Poshmark, cater to a specific audience, and often offer the best return on investment for your footwear. Poshmark also offers free shipping and gives you a pre-paid shipping label for your purchases.

The process for selling sneakers online can be complex and full of fees. Many online platforms charge hefty fees, but if you want to sell your Yeezys or Air Jordans, you can do so safely. Listed below are three places to sell sneakers online. There are also hundreds of local and regional stores that accept sneaker-related purchases. Some online auction sites even provide free shipping and payment services, though these can take some time.

The best way to get the most money from your sneaker is to price it correctly. The older the sneaker is, the more valuable it becomes. This means that you should price it at a price that reflects the market value and leaves room for further price cuts. If possible, you can post your sneakers in Facebook buying and selling groups or forums. But before posting your sneakers for sale, do some research and learn as much as you can about its history and its market value.

Another place to sell your sneakers is through GOAT, a site that accepts sneakers and apparel. The platform allows you to sell sneakers with their box intact. GOAT also accepts sneakers from top brands. So, if you don't want to spend a lot of time searching through websites, Flight Club may be the best option. However, make sure your sneakers are in pristine condition and are free of defects.

The most popular and easy-to-use marketplace to sell your sneakers is Kixify. The platform is available for Android and iOS devices, and there's no charge to list your sneakers. The service also allows you to customize your store to sell your sneakers. You can add as many listings as you'd like. Kixify's platform is the largest online sneaker marketplace, offering hundreds of brands and styles. Kixify doesn't charge fees to list your sneakers, so it's definitely worth checking out.

In addition to eBay, you can also try Stadium Goods. Located in New York City, this store accepts consignment sneakers. You can ship your shoes directly to the company, or drop them off at one of their Market Centers. It pays eighty percent of the list price and pays you once a week. To sell your sneakers with Stadium Goods, you must fill out a W9 form.

Crossroads Trading has more than thirty locations nationwide, but the only drawback is the steep commission. Selling shoes on Poshmark will earn you $2.95 per sale, which isn't worth much if you don't plan to sell them. However, if you're looking for cash for your old shoes, you should check out Crossroads Trading. This consignment store also offers up to 50% store credit for your shoes.

Selling Sneakers on Poshmark

When selling sneakers, it's best to include as many pictures as possible. Poshmark has a limit of 12 photos per item, so take a few different angles of each pair. Include the tags, labels, and even close-ups to show any flaws. Poshmark will give you a few days to accept an offer. After accepting the offer, you can ship the sneakers or accept a lower price.

Poshmark sizes are determined by the average size of the general population. The more common a size, the higher the chances of selling the item. According to the latest study, the average American woman wears sizes 16-18. Unlike the usual belief, however, the 16-18 size is the most likely to sell. As such, you'll want to offer sneakers that are similar in size. Using the "StockX" feature on Poshmark will help you see how much sneakers are selling for on the site. This feature will help you see how much each pair is worth and determine the best resell price.

Listed items on Poshmark can range anywhere from $10 to thousands of dollars. It's free to list, and Poshmark allows you to list unlimited items. If you sell a few pairs, you can make a decent profit. Those who sell sneakers on Poshmark usually earn more than they paid for the pair. However, some sellers are disappointed with the lack of interest. If you are one of those people, selling sneakers on Poshmark can be a fun and profitable experience.

As with any other site, Poshmark prohibits the sale of counterfeit products and unauthorized replicas. Members who try to sell counterfeit or knockoff items risk being permanently banned from the site. This is especially true for sneakers. It's also illegal to list items that are prohibited by law. Likewise, you shouldn't sell items that are derived from endangered species, or those that require a prescription. Selling shoes and accessories that fall under these categories will only make your listings unappealing to potential buyers.

Remember to put yourself in the shoes of your customers

when selling sneakers. They may not know when they'll need the same pair again and might not be interested in spending that much money. It's always better to make a profit than to lose it all. If your sneakers don't fit the bill, try selling them on another website. You'll likely get a better sale this way. So don't let them walk away from your shoes.

While Poshmark has a huge community of users, you should be realistic when pricing your items. Make sure you are willing to price your sneakers appropriately. Remember that buyers are looking for a bargain. Often times, that means matching other sellers' prices. This takes away some of your profit. Beware of scammers. When you're not willing to match your buyers' prices, you won't get any.

Selling Sneakers on ThredUP and Poshmark

If you're tired of storing your unused sneakers, consider selling them on thredUP. You can sell your used sneakers for cash and earn a nice return. You'll also receive a prepaid shipping label and receive payment through PayPal or direct deposit. The process is simple and fast, and thredUP's 90+ expert team will evaluate your sneakers and get you paid within a few days.

You can also list your secondhand sneakers on Poshmark. This website or app makes it easy to list your sneakers in less than 30 seconds. Unlike other marketplaces, thredUP accepts all types of footwear - men's, women's, and children's. The only items you can't sell on thredUP are undergarments, sleepwear, and jewelry. You can list your sneakers on Poshmark for free, too.

Poshmark stores all inventory, and thredUP keeps them for 60-90 days depending on the brand. However, if you've accidentally listed a pair of sneakers that are too old to be worn, you can still reclaim the shoes and get paid for them! Just make sure you reclaim the items within seven days before they expire, because after that time, they belong to thredUP. Also, thredUP no longer allows sellers to use their points to receive free shipping on their orders.

There are many other ways to sell your used sneakers. Aside from selling sneakers on thredUP., you can also try Craigslist. You can post free ads there and find buyers in your local area. Be sure to post photos of your sneakers and provide details about your shoes. You can also use Poshmark, a fashion resale app, to list your sneakers for sale. As long as the seller meets all of the requirements, Poshmark allows you to make a small profit selling sneakers online.

Reselling apparel is a lucrative business and the market for second-hand clothing is growing rapidly. Reselling apparel will increase by 11x over the next five years, according to thredUP.com. To sell your used sneakers on thredUP, you need to have a clean-out kit. ThredUP will mail you the clean-out bag once you've finished cleaning them. They accept up to fifteen pounds of clothing in a package, so the shipping cost is very low.

    Reselling online makes selling shoes more affordable than ever. While thredUP does require a minimal amount of preparation, you can also be hands-off. If you're hands-on, you can make a spreadsheet of your items, take pictures of them to prevent any damage, and check the processing dates and reclaim dates. If you're hands-off, you can avoid all of the hassle of checking the items to make sure they're received. However, if you're a hands-off seller, you may want to take pictures to protect your items and make sure that they sell quickly.

Selling Sneakers on The RealReal

If you are selling your sneakers on The RealReal, you need to know some basics before you start listing the shoes. To avoid making mistakes, use saved searches and obsessions to keep track of your favorite items. Saved searches are also good for remembering keyword phrases that may catch people's attention. RealReal posts new items twice a day, at 10am and 7pm EST. So you might want to check back on the site at these times to see what items are being sold for.

To start your listing, first visit Rebag.com, a French online shoe exchange that ships items worldwide. Select the type of shoe you want to sell, and then fill out the details of the shoes. Add pictures if possible. Once the shoes are listed, you can start collecting money. The commission is 10% of the selling price. You can also sell shoes that you no longer wear but are still in good condition.

The RealReal website is easy to navigate. You can also browse shoes by price range and popularity. The RealReal website lists shoes by popularity, which means more potential buyers are looking for specific items. Using this website to find new sneakers can help you make a profit. You can even get paid if your sneakers sell for more than what you expect. However, you need to be aware of the fact that reselling online is not without its flaws. The prices are high for pre-owned items.

The RealReal has released its list of the top-selling men's sneakers. The Achilles low-top, an Italian leather sneaker, is the best selling men's sneaker on The RealReal. The Buscemi 100MM, a luxury sneaker influenced by handbags, is the second-best-selling shoe on the site. Finally, the Balenciaga Arena high-top is the third-best-selling men's shoe on The RealReal.

Another good way to make money selling sneakers is StockX. While better known for its website, StockX recently released an app. It is currently the 17th-most-used app in this demographic. Limited-edition sneaker releases can be worth up to $3,000 on StockX. By listing these shoes on the site, you can sell them for up to three times their retail value! This marketplace works like a stock market, with real-time feedback from fellow users and accurate resell prices.

Air Maxes are popular on The RealReal. The RealReal currently has hundreds of Air Maxes for sale, including several signed by Eminem. Eminem's Eminem x Nike Air Max 97, which was released in 2006, has been sold in less than 24 hours! One of the most popular sneakers on The RealReal is an Eminem x Nike Air Max 97, which was released in 2006 with a Shady Records logo and a blue Air Max unit. It also has an inscription signed by Marshall.

Selling Sneakers on Flyp

Flyp.com is an online marketplace where you can sell your sneakers. You can receive a payment via PayPal, Venmo, Cash App, or Apple Pay. Payment times vary and depend on shipping times and the pro seller's ability to find a buyer. On average, your items should sell within three months. Listed on the website for free, sellers can receive up to $350 for their products. You can sell sneakers in any style you like.

If you'd rather sell a pair of sneakers on your own, you can use the website to find a Pro Seller. This seller can then take the photos and set the price. You'll receive a percentage of the sale. Flyp connects you with Pro Sellers who specialize in the brand you're selling. You'll earn commission from each sale and get paid each time the item sells. Flyp has many more ways to make money selling sneakers.

Flyp has a great reputation for paying top dollar for quality shoes. They also offer free shipping labels, so you can send a pair of sneakers to a potential buyer. Flyp also offers a protection policy. If your shoes are damaged or do not sell, you can contact a Flyp Pro Seller to get your money. Flyp guarantees you'll get paid. The only catch? The process is a bit confusing.

Before you list your sneakers for sale, make sure the sneakers are clean and presentable. Make sure to post multiple listings on the site. This way, you'll increase the likelihood of a quick sale. Don't forget to upload a picture of your sneakers so they will look their best. There are several other websites where you can sell your sneakers. Check out Poshmark, which is another popular resale app.

While selling sneakers on eBay is not a new idea, many people are finding success with it. The website is free to sign up and allows sellers to post their listings. Once approved, sellers can choose to ship their sneakers to their buyers, with verified shipping. The sellers pay Kixify a commission of 10% of the total sales price. You can also list your sneakers on

GOAT, an online platform that allows you to order prepaid shipping labels.

The process is simple and free - once you have an account, you can upload your sneakers, write a description, and set the price. You can even "like" your items on social media to get more exposure. You can even ship your sneakers yourself, with a prepaid shipping label and a tracking number. You can also choose to sell your sneakers through the Buffalo Exchange. It will be much easier and more profitable than ever before.

The selling process on Heroine is similar to that of Grailed. You can use your Grailed login credentials to sign up for Heroine. Kixify is another free website for selling sneakers. It focuses on casual as well as collector-grade sneakers. Unlike Grailed, Kixify does not require a storefront, and you can list your sneakers without any costs. You will be charged a 8% commission when your item sells.

How to Make Money Selling Shoes Online

There are many advantages of buying and selling your own heels at buyMYheels.com. You will earn between 50 and 55 percent of the selling price. Depending on how many pairs you sell, you may receive your cash directly into your bank account or by check. You can sell your shoes anywhere in the world, and the site has a global network of buyers. You won't have to pay a commission, although it does charge a listing fee of $7. This site also has strict guidelines for non-name-brand items.

Another benefit of buyMYheels.com is that it's free to sign up, and it accepts almost any type of used item. You can sell anything from your old sneakers to new clothes and electronics. All you have to do is post a picture and a description of your shoes, and you'll receive payment within three days. You can also choose to pay the buyer through store credit. However, there's a catch. The site doesn't pay shipping costs, so you might be better off trying out Mercari instead.

Sell your used shoes: Another popular online platform to sell shoes is ThredUp. Unlike eBay, ThredUp will pay you a fee to list your shoes on the site. In return, you'll be paid via PayPal, Stripe, or shopping credit. eBay is the classic online marketplace to sell used goods and has a wide range of features. With a small fee, you can sell shoes and accessories and earn a good profit.

If you're looking for sneakers, Grailed has a wide variety of popular brands. While Grailed isn't as popular as buyMYheels.com, it is the best place for people to buy and sell designer sneakers. It pays via PayPal, so you won't have to worry about transferring money from your bank account. Just remember to choose your market carefully and wait for approval. You'll sell shoes faster if you use quality images.

Shipping costs are low and simple with Mercari. You can either purchase a pre-paid shipping label or pay the seller's postage costs directly. If you have a large collection of heels, you can choose to send them to yourself at a discounted rate, saving yourself money on postage. You'll be notified when your item sells and you'll receive a pre-packaged shipping kit. Once your item sells, you'll be paid through PayPal or a prepaid debit card.

When selling online, it's important to remember that some scams are common and will cause you a lot of trouble. Kixify is an option for you if you're selling your sneakers in your local area. The seller gets a percentage of the sales and Kixify keeps a hefty 8% commission. The site also allows you to meet buyers in person. There are many people who have sold their sneakers for more than a few hundred dollars on buyMYheels.com.

There are many ways to sell your shoes. You can sell your shoes for cash at Buffalo Exchange. All you have to do is list your shoes on the site, provide an excellent description and set a reasonable asking price. If your shoes are a good quality condition, you'll be able to sell them for much more than you would have expected to. The site offers a number of opportunities for selling your shoes, but you must remember to use good judgment when dealing with buyers.

Tips For Buying on the Kixify Marketplace

The most common reason why people get scammed on Kixify is due to sellers. However, the company does pay attention to unsuccessful transactions, and refunds people who use Paypal. Also, never provide more information than you need to get the product you're looking for. Moreover, real sellers will let you know that their items have been delivered. The following are some tips for buying on Kixify:

Sign up for Kixify with a PayPal account. Once you've set up your account, you'll be able to begin selling sneakers on the site. You'll need a PayPal address to get paid. You'll be required to accept Kixify's terms and conditions before you can post your products on the website. Once you've done this, you'll be ready to list your products on the Kixify website.

Set up an account on Kixify for free. There are no set-up or monthly fees, and anyone can sign up. There are, however, some downsides to using Kixify, as it's possible to get scammed by third-party sellers. If you're concerned about the safety of your purchases, you'll be glad to know that Kixify offers refunds in case of scams. In addition, you can easily check whether you've been scammed through Kixify if you've been scammed.

While kixify is free to sign up for, there are plenty of scammers out there. If you've had your heart broken by scammers, you should try out Kixify first. It's the best way to get started selling on the online marketplace. Aside from that, Kixify also allows you to make extra money on the side! You'll be surprised at the vast amount of products and services available.

After signing up, you can browse the available items on Kixify. You'll be able to see their detailed descriptions, shipping costs, and total price. You can choose from various sizes and price ranges. It's easy to check the authenticity of the shoes that you've found by using Kixify. Once you're done, you can upload photos of the shoes you're selling on the app. Kixify also offers mobile apps to help you sell on the site.

    Besides Kixify, eBay is another alternative. The online auction site is controversial, but it offers many categories with reasonably used or refurbished items. It's a trusted website with millions of users all over the world. Another similar site is GOAT, which offers AfterPay payments so that you can pay for sneakers in installments. It also offers buyer feedback and seller FAQ. Aside from that, Kixify offers a number of features to its users.

How to Sell Sneakers to Grailed

Depending on your location, Grailed has two options for shipping your sneakers. You can either charge a flat rate of $1.99 or take the extra step of offering a percentage of the selling price. You can also sell multiple pairs of sneakers at once. Once you get a payment, Grailed will send you an email letting you know when your sneakers have been shipped. In either case, you'll need to pay the shipping charges.

Before selling your sneakers, you'll need to set up an account on Grailed. You'll want to link your PayPal account to your Grailed account. Next, you'll need to upload 3 high-quality photos of the sneakers for sale. These pictures will help your listing stand out and make potential buyers click your link. Grailed also provides a shipping label printing service if you have a printer. Once you've uploaded a photo of the sneakers you'd like to sell, you'll want to make sure you've included a tagged description.

Once you've accepted a buyer's offer, Grailed will release funds to your PayPal account. However, if you're selling sneakers that are no longer in good condition or without a tracking number, Grailed may hold onto the funds. If you've shipped the sneakers and sent them via mail, the funds will be released to your account within three days. If you're a new seller, this may take a little longer. Sometimes, PayPal asks for more information or verification.

Once you've created an account on Grailed, you can upload photos of the shoes that you want to sell. You can also tag each photo with your username so that the buyers know who you're selling to. Be sure to take several photos so that they show multiple angles and ensure the quality of the product. Lastly, ship your sneakers as soon as possible! There's no reason why you shouldn't try it!

One last advantage of Grailed is their money-back guarantee. If the item doesn't arrive in a timely fashion or is a fake, buyers can receive a full refund. Grailed users can also rate the packaging of the sneakers to see if it's clean and presentable. If you have questions about whether your sneakers are authentic, make sure to contact the seller directly before buying them. Besides, you'll also be able to view the ratings of each seller so you can make a wise decision when selling your sneakers.

When selling your sneakers, you need to keep in mind that your buyer may be skeptical of your low price. You should also consider shipping costs in the listing. You can add this cost to the price if you'd like to, but keep in mind that shipping costs are often a determining factor in the decision of buyers. If the buyer isn't comfortable paying this much, don't worry. Keeping clear communication will help your deal go smoothly.

eBay is another option for selling your sneakers. While the popularity of Grailed has decreased over the years, eBay is still an excellent option for selling sneakers online. eBay users often add hyped suffixes to their listings. Unlike Grailed, these users are typically older and more experienced. So if you don't want to waste your time selling on eBay, try Grailed. It's a simple and straightforward way to sell sneakers online.

Selling Sneakers and Streetwear on StockX

If you're a sneaker or streetwear fan, you've probably already heard of StockX. The selling site was founded in 2015 and focuses on a niche market: hype footwear. The goal was to give fans an easy way to buy and sell their favorite shoes. Users can buy and sell their sneakers with just a click, and all of the transactions are secure.

While it is possible to sell just about anything on this site, you should be aware of its limitations. For one thing, StockX only lists items that the company has uploaded, so you may not find rare or limited edition sneakers on the site. And, because all items are authenticated, they may take weeks or months to arrive. The longer they take, the higher the cost. You'll also have to pay for delivery fees and duties, which can add a significant markup to the price.

In order to sell items on StockX, you'll need to list them on the site. Once the listing is live, you'll need to send the item to an authentication center or drop it off in a physical location. You can also set a price for your items on StockX, and you can purchase them instantly. If you're looking for more, you can also place bids. To sell your sneakers on StockX, you'll need to supply payment information. The selling process can take several weeks, so it's important to have a high minimum budget.

Founded in 2015, StockX is the easiest and most secure way to buy and sell sneakers. The company has a reputation for authenticity, which is key when buying high-end sneakers. It has over eight hundred employees and offices in the United Kingdom and Netherlands. With its unique platform, users can buy and sell shoes at discounted prices. The average score is 3.4/5, and reviews are posted every day.

In 2016, Dan Gilbert, the founder of Quicken Loans, a major tech investor, backed StockX and its IPO. Gilbert recognized

Luber's work at Campless and decided to invest in StockX. Gilbert and Schwartz partnered together to create StockX. While the company is growing, Dan Gilbert continues to be invested in the company. In the coming years, StockX plans to expand internationally.

Like eBay, StockX has a strict quality control policy. Customers should check for authenticity before buying and selling on the site. All products must be authentic to avoid fakes and scams. A good way to avoid scammers is to sign up for a StockX membership. The site is also worth checking out if you're looking for sneakers. StockX has an excellent reputation.

As the world becomes more expensive, StockX is seeing rapid growth. Its focus on this niche helped it land a $3.8 billion valuation in April. Despite its relatively small size, StockX is expanding fast and has ambitious plans. In addition to selling sneakers, the company is expanding into other categories such as handbags, electronics and even clothing. So, it's safe to say that the future looks bright for StockX.

GOAT Review - A Review of GOAT, a Sneaker-focused Shoe Resale Website

GOAT, a sneaker-focused shoe re-sale website, started as a site where the sneaker community could buy and sell new and used kicks. Today, it is a legitimate market worth over $3.7 billion. Unlike other online marketplaces, GOAT's staff works closely with sellers to make sure that the shoes they are selling are authentic. Its low commission rate helps it compete with other online marketplaces and a wide selection of sneakers.

GOAT has helped the sneaker industry flourish, bringing in more demand and hype to previously unsold sneakers. GOAT is run by Eddy Lu and Daishin Sugano, two college friends who decided to create the website after purchasing a pair of fake Air Jordan 5 Grapes on eBay. Fake sneakers are a big problem in the sneaker industry. It is estimated that up to 90% of shoes are fake, including Nike, the most popular brand.

GOAT is a sneaker-centric shoe resale website that uses a combination of digital authentication, machine learning, and image recognition to identify authentic sneakers. The website allows users to search for and buy rare sneakers online, and connects them with like-minded individuals. With its image recognition and machine learning technology, GOAT helps sellers list their shoes, as well as get accurate pricing information in real time.

GOAT charges a seller fee for transactions. The fee is based on where you live, but it can be as low as $5 if you are based in the United States. Sellers can get their payout through PayPal or direct deposit. They are also a good alternative to StockX, but GOAT offers the best value for money. It has been around for a decade and has become a huge hit in the sneaker community.

GOAT Group has raised over $100 million in financing, making it a billion-dollar company with physical retail stores and an online app. The company also recently reported that it has doubled its user base from the last year to more than seven million. This growth demonstrates the huge potential of the sneaker-focused shoe resale market. It is estimated that the global sneaker market is expected to reach $30 billion by 2030.

GOAT offers the lowest fees, which is great news for those looking for a secondhand pair of sneakers. In the near term, GOAT is predicted to sell more Yeezys than Adidas, so you can be sure that you can get a great deal on your new sneakers. But before you purchase your new pair, take a look at its pricing strategy.

While GOAT focuses on reselling second-hand sneakers, it also sells cleaned sneakers through a separate site called GOAT Clean. The GOAT Clean site photographs the shoes and offers a guarantee of authenticity. GOAT was launched in 2012, but it only recently merged with the retail giant Flight Club, which runs three flagship stores in New York and Los Angeles. The new company plans to expand its reach by integrating its stores and mobile apps.

Selling Sneakers on Heroine

The process of selling sneakers on Heroine. is the same as selling sneakers on Grailed, but you'll have more luck selling women's clothing on Heroine. You'll have to pay a 6% commission on each item sold, plus PayPal's 2.9% domestic and 4.4% international fees. If you've ever sold clothing on Grailed, you'll understand how it works. In addition, you'll get more exposure for your sneakers on Heroine, as more women use it than any other site.

Craigslist is another option for selling sneakers online. It was one of the first online marketplaces, but over time, it's gotten a bad rap. While it can be a great place to sell sneakers, there are many flaws in Craigslist, and scammers are abundant. Also, Craigslist is not as secure as other marketplace sites, so you have to make sure that the buyer is reputable and safe.

Mercari has a comprehensive listing feature and does not charge a listing fee. Instead, it takes 10% of the total sale, and offers a prepaid shipping label if you choose to ship your shoes yourself. The service also has a customer feedback feature, and lets buyers "like" your items on social media. When selling sneakers on Mercari, use a tracking number and include an accurate address. This way, you'll receive a full payment faster than you would on other sites.

In addition to selling shoes online, Mercari has a buyer's forum that will give you valuable feedback. This forum allows buyers to connect with sellers in their community and buy and sell sneakers. Unlike eBay, Mercari has a no-commission policy for selling name-brand sneakers. Moreover, the site also has strict policies against the sale of replicas and unknown name brands. You may also sell other items on Mercari if you want to make a profit with your online sales.

Another great alternative to selling sneakers on Heroine. is 5 Miles. This site is dedicated to streetwear and sneakers, but is not exclusively geared toward sneakers. You can sell a pair of sneakers by uploading it to the site, setting a price, and writing a description. Once a sale is made, you can communicate with the buyer directly through the app, and even meet up in person. The app is available for Android and iOS devices.

Once you have an account, you can start listing your shoes for sale. Some platforms will let you list your shoes for free, but if they pull your product due to compliance issues, you'll lose your chance at free listing. You must also post pictures of your shoes, showing them in the best possible light. It's important to provide photos that show any defects or flaws. This will help customers make an informed decision about whether or not to purchase your sneakers.

Selling Sneakers on Tradesy

Tradesy is an online marketplace for authentic designer fashion. Once you sign up, you will receive constant messages from real buyers and sellers. The website also gives you a free shipping kit to send out your sneakers to interested buyers. Tradesy will handle returns and issues with payment. Selling sneakers on Tradesy is a great way to earn a lot of money. However, be sure to choose the right platform to sell your sneakers.

Before selling on eBay, make sure that you place the items in the right category and provide a full description. Usually, the more information you provide to your potential buyers, the higher your chances of selling. You should also include up to four photographs of your sneakers in your listing. To ensure that your shoes receive the best photos, view the Shoe Photography Guide. Your photos should be smaller than 4 MB in size. After you've uploaded photos, set a price that is realistic and achievable for the shoes. Be ready to negotiate with buyers. If the customer is willing to pay a bit less than what you've set for your sneakers, then you'll have a higher chance of selling them.

If you're selling shoes, you'll want to make sure you ship the shoes as soon as possible. Tradesy allows you to request a prepaid shipping label or ship the shoes yourself. If you're shipping the items yourself, be sure to include a tracking number in the packaging. Once a buyer buys your sneakers, they have 3 days to submit a review. If they don't, they can simply leave a positive feedback. If they're happy with their purchase, you can receive payment by direct deposit. For payments under $10, you'll need to pay a $2 fee.

Nike and Other Sneakers Are Made in China

The production of sneakers in Chinese factories is a booming business, so why don't more brands consider this as a possible location for their manufacturing operations? Despite the low cost of labor in China, you can still find excellent factories for your production needs. Take a look at the following factories in the country to find out how they produce these shoes. Listed below are some of their key features and capabilities. If you're interested in purchasing Chinese sneakers, you can also check out their website.

The working conditions in these factories can be hazardous, too. Despite the low wages, workers were frequently exposed to dust and fumes. One worker died after inhaling toxic chemicals. Noise pollution, hot weather, and congestion were common workplace hazards at the Nike factory. Employees complained of skin irritations, dizziness, and headaches. Several were also afflicted with respiratory problems. Despite their injuries, many workers felt that their employers did not care about their health.

Most of the famous sneakers are made in China. However, lesser-known brands also make them. There are factories in Xiamen and Shenzhen that manufacture a variety of different footwear products. Not all shoes are produced in one factory. Some are made in Vietnam or Mongolia and assembled in another location. Some factories only manufacture specific components and then assemble them in another factory. For those looking for high quality sneakers, there are many places you can find them.

While you can visit shoe factories in China for wholesale purchases, it is recommended to check the country's trade shows to find the best quality suppliers. These trade shows are where many manufacturers come to meet potential customers and suppliers. You'll also learn more about quality control and the latest trends in the footwear industry. There are a lot of advantages and disadvantages to choosing a factory in China, so it's crucial to get a good supplier.

One of the most significant issues that you may encounter is the lack of worker's rights. Although you are not allowed to join a trade union at Nike factories, you can speak to a supervisor in your locality to raise your concerns. But you should consider that you may end up losing your job if you complain. One factory employee was fired after complaining about the conditions at his workplace. This is an unfortunate outcome, but the situation makes us wonder if these factories really care about the rights of their workers.

Converse is another example of a brand that has suffered. The brand used to operate a huge plant in Lumberton, NC to produce sneakers. Converse made shoes in the US until 2001, but the company filed for bankruptcy and shut down its manufacturing plants. In the following years, Nike bought Converse and the plants closed down. Today, many of the brands produced in China were made in the USA. In fact, some of the most famous brands of sneakers came from the USA.

Unmasking the Authenticity: A Comprehensive Guide to Sneaker Authentication and Counterfeit Detection

Sneaker culture has become a global phenomenon, with avid enthusiasts and collectors constantly seeking out the latest releases and rare editions. However, this popularity has also given rise to an alarming surge in counterfeit sneakers flooding the market. The need for sneaker authentication and counterfeit detection has never been more crucial. In this comprehensive chapter, we will delve into the intricacies of sneaker authentication, exploring the methods and techniques used to determine the genuineness of sneakers and spot counterfeit replicas.

Understanding the Stakes:

The sneaker market, particularly the resale market, is valued at billions of dollars. Counterfeit sneakers pose significant risks to consumers, ranging from financial losses to potential health hazards from substandard materials. Recognizing the importance of authenticating sneakers helps protect buyers from falling victim to counterfeit schemes.

Key Authentication Elements:

Authenticating sneakers involves examining various elements that distinguish genuine products from counterfeits. These elements include:

a) Branding and Logo: Genuine sneakers exhibit precise, consistent, and accurate branding elements, including logos, fonts, and placement.

b) Materials and Construction: Authentic sneakers are crafted with high-quality materials and showcase superior craftsmanship, while counterfeit replicas may have noticeable flaws, such as poor stitching or cheap materials.

c) Packaging and Labels: Authentic sneakers are accompanied by original packaging, including labels, tags, and boxes. Examining the quality, design, and printing details of these components can help verify authenticity.

d) Serial Numbers and QR Codes: Many sneaker manufacturers incorporate unique serial numbers or QR codes on their products to enable traceability. Validating these codes through official sources can confirm authenticity.

Official Retail Channels:

Purchasing sneakers from authorized retailers or reputable resellers significantly reduces the risk of encountering counterfeit products. Official retail channels provide a higher level of assurance regarding authenticity, as they source directly from the brand.

Third-Party Authentication Services:

To combat the counterfeit market, specialized third-party authentication services have emerged. These services employ experts who scrutinize sneakers using their in-depth knowledge and expertise. By leveraging their experience and access to authentic references, they provide a reliable and unbiased opinion on the legitimacy of sneakers.

Online Resources and Communities:

The digital realm has become a valuable resource for sneaker authentication. Numerous online communities, forums, and social media platforms are dedicated to sharing authentication tips, identifying replicas, and exposing counterfeit sellers. Engaging with these communities can help individuals enhance their authentication skills.

Physical Examination Techniques:

Authentication often involves a physical examination of the sneakers. Some common techniques include:

a) Stitching and Glue: Inspecting the stitching quality and glue application can reveal telltale signs of counterfeit sneakers, as authentic pairs boast clean, precise workmanship.

b) Materials and Textures: Comparing the texture, feel, and quality of materials against known authentic samples can help detect discrepancies.

c) Colorways and Shades: Counterfeit sneakers may exhibit inconsistencies in color shades, often noticeable when compared to genuine versions.

d) Weight and Balance: Authentic sneakers tend to have consistent weight distribution and balanced design, whereas replicas may feel lighter or imbalanced.

Brand-Specific Authentication Guides:

Major sneaker brands often release official authentication guides to educate consumers about their specific authentication features. These guides highlight unique details, construction methods, and branding elements that counterfeiters often struggle to replicate.

Technology-Driven Solutions:

Innovative technologies are playing an increasingly vital role in sneaker authentication. Brands are exploring the use of NFC chips, QR codes, and blockchain to enable secure product verification, providing consumers with instant access to a sneaker's authentication history and origin.

As sneaker culture continues to flourish, so does the prevalence of counterfeit sneakers. To protect themselves from financial losses and potential harm, buyers must equip themselves with knowledge and expertise in sneaker authentication. By understanding the key authentication elements, engaging with reliable retail channels and online communities, leveraging third-party authentication services, and employing physical examination techniques, sneaker enthusiasts can confidently navigate the market while safeguarding their investments. Remember, the true essence of the sneaker culture lies in the authenticity and uniqueness of each pair, and it is our collective responsibility to ensure that this essence remains untainted by counterfeits.

Sneaker Release Strategies and the Phenomenon of Drop Culture: An In-depth Analysis

In recent years, the world of sneakers has evolved into a cultural phenomenon with a dedicated following of enthusiasts, collectors, and resellers. Sneaker releases have become highly anticipated events, often accompanied by a frenzy of hype, limited supply, and exclusive marketing strategies.

Sneaker Release Strategies:

1.1. Limited Editions and Collaborations:

One of the most common strategies employed by sneaker brands is the production of limited-edition releases and collaborations. By partnering with influential designers, artists, musicians, or athletes, brands can generate buzz and create a sense of exclusivity. Limited releases instill a sense of scarcity and encourage consumers to act swiftly to secure a pair.

1.2. Teasers and Sneak Peeks:

Brands often utilize teasers and sneak peeks to build anticipation and generate hype around upcoming releases. Through social media, promotional videos, or exclusive leaks, companies create a sense of excitement and curiosity, fueling the desire for the sneakers among enthusiasts.

1.3. Raffles and Lottery Systems:

To combat the issues associated with traditional "first-come, first-served" release methods, many brands have adopted raffle or lottery systems. These approaches level the playing field, ensuring that everyone has an equal chance to purchase the sneakers, regardless of their geographical location or internet connection speed.

1.4. Retailer Collaborations:

Brands frequently collaborate with specific retailers to

release their sneakers exclusively through those channels. This strategy helps both parties by driving traffic to the retailer and increasing the appeal and desirability of the brand's products. Retailer collaborations often lead to long queues and camping outside stores, contributing to the overall hype and excitement.

The Emergence of Drop Culture:

2.1. Defining Drop Culture:

Drop culture refers to the phenomenon surrounding limited sneaker releases, characterized by intense hype, limited supply, and high demand. Sneaker drops create a sense of urgency and competition among consumers, with the goal of being one of the lucky few to secure a pair. The scarcity and exclusivity associated with drops fuel the desire and obsession surrounding coveted sneakers.

2.2. Online Exclusive Releases:

The rise of e-commerce and online platforms has revolutionized sneaker releases. Many brands now opt for online-exclusive releases, leveraging digital platforms to reach a global audience and streamline the purchasing process. However, the shift to online releases has also given rise to various challenges, such as website crashes, bots, and reseller dominance.

2.3. Reseller Culture:

Drop culture has given birth to a thriving reseller market, where individuals purchase limited-edition sneakers with the sole intention of reselling them at inflated prices. Resellers leverage the scarcity of certain releases to capitalize on the high demand and turn a profit. This resale culture has led to increased prices, reduced accessibility for genuine consumers, and ethical concerns within the sneaker community.

Impact on Consumer Behavior:

3.1. Hype and Brand Loyalty:

Drop culture and limited sneaker releases foster an environment of hype and exclusivity. This leads to heightened brand loyalty, with consumers actively seeking out the latest releases and participating in the culture surrounding their favorite brands. Sneakerheads often display their collections as status symbols, contributing to a sense of identity and community.

3.2. Emotional Connection:

Sneaker releases are not just about the product itself; they often evoke emotional connections and personal narratives. Whether it's nostalgia for a retro release or admiration for an athlete or artist associated with a collaboration, consumers form deep attachments to certain sneakers. Brands capitalize on this emotional connection to create compelling marketing campaigns and further fuel the demand.

3.3. Frustration and Consumer Fatigue:

While drop culture can be thrilling for those lucky enough to secure highly sought-after releases, it also generates frustration and consumer fatigue. Constantly competing against bots, encountering website crashes, and missing out on desired pairs can lead to disappointment and disillusionment among consumers. This frustration can result in decreased enthusiasm or even a shift towards other brands or hobbies.

Sneaker release strategies and drop culture have transformed the sneaker industry, turning it into a thriving market driven by scarcity, hype, and exclusivity. The strategies employed by brands to create demand and anticipation have given rise to a dedicated community of enthusiasts, collectors, and resellers. However, the phenomenon of drop culture has also sparked debates surrounding accessibility, ethical concerns, and the impact on genuine consumers. As the sneaker industry continues to evolve, it is essential for brands to strike a balance between exclusivity and inclusivity, ensuring that the culture remains vibrant, diverse, and accessible to all who appreciate the artistry and craftsmanship of sneakers.

Sneaker Collaborations and Limited Editions: A Revolution in Footwear Culture

Sneaker collaborations and limited editions have become a phenomenon in the world of footwear, capturing the hearts of sneaker enthusiasts and fashion enthusiasts alike. This unique fusion of fashion, art, and popular culture has transformed the sneaker industry, elevating it to new heights of creativity, exclusivity, and collectability.

The Rise of Sneaker Collaborations:

1.1 Evolution of Sneaker Culture: Sneakers have evolved from functional athletic shoes to iconic symbols of style, self-expression, and cultural identity. The emergence of sneaker culture paved the way for collaborations as a means to bring together diverse creative forces and cater to the growing demand for unique footwear.

1.2 Creative Fusion: Sneaker collaborations represent a fusion of different industries, combining the expertise of sneaker brands with the artistic vision of designers, musicians, athletes, artists, and even luxury fashion houses. This dynamic synergy leads to the birth of limited-edition sneakers that transcend conventional boundaries.

Impact and Significance:

2.1 Cultural Significance: Sneaker collaborations reflect the evolving intersection between fashion, art, sports, and popular culture. These partnerships often result in designs that encapsulate historical references, social commentary, and personal narratives, resonating with sneaker enthusiasts on a deeper level.

2.2 Brand Awareness and Market Expansion: Collaborations provide sneaker brands with a platform to tap into new markets and demographics. By partnering with influential figures and brands outside the sneaker industry, companies can extend their reach and create hype, ultimately driving sales and brand loyalty.

2.3 Resale Market and Investment Value: Limited-edition sneakers are highly sought after, creating a vibrant resale market. Sneaker collaborations have turned sneakers into valuable commodities, with some rare pairs fetching exorbitant prices. This has opened up new opportunities for collectors and investors to capitalize on the value of these collaborative creations.

Notable Sneaker Collaborations:

3.1 Nike and Off-White: The partnership between Nike and fashion designer Virgil Abloh's brand, Off-White, has revolutionized sneaker collaborations. Their "The Ten" collection, featuring deconstructed designs and signature branding, sparked immense hype and set new trends in the sneaker industry.

3.2 Adidas and Kanye West: The collaboration between Adidas and rapper-turned-designer Kanye West resulted in the creation of the highly popular Yeezy line. These sneakers have become synonymous with exclusivity, innovation, and urban fashion.

3.3 Puma and Rihanna: Puma's partnership with pop icon Rihanna led to the creation of the Fenty Puma collection, blending high fashion with streetwear. This collaboration pushed boundaries, empowering women and embracing diversity in sneaker culture.

3.4 Converse and Comme des Garçons: Converse, known for its iconic Chuck Taylor All Star, joined forces with avant-garde fashion brand Comme des Garçons to create unique and bold designs that challenged traditional sneaker aesthetics.

Sneaker Collaborations as Artistic Expression:

4.1 Limited-Edition Artwork: Sneaker collaborations often blur the line between footwear and art. Some collaborations feature intricate details, custom prints, premium materials, and even hand-painted elements, transforming sneakers into wearable masterpieces.

4.2 Collaborative Creative Processes: Sneaker collaborations involve an intensive creative process that combines the vision, expertise, and distinctive styles of both parties. Designers and brands collaborate closely, resulting in innovative and unconventional sneakers that push the boundaries of design.

The Future of Sneaker Collaborations:

5.1 Sustainability and Conscious Collaborations: As sustainability becomes an increasingly important focus, sneaker collaborations are expected to align with ethical practices, using eco-friendly materials, and promoting conscious consumption.

5.2 Emerging Collaborative Partnerships: Sneaker collaborations are likely to expand beyond the realms of fashion, art, and sports. We can anticipate unique partnerships between sneaker brands and tech companies, musicians, gaming franchises, and even space exploration enterprises.

5.3 Technological Advancements: Sneaker collaborations might incorporate cutting-edge technologies, such as 3D printing, smart fabrics, and interactive elements, further blurring the lines between fashion, technology, and innovation.

Sneaker collaborations and limited editions have revolutionized the sneaker industry, elevating sneakers from functional footwear to coveted works of art. These collaborations transcend traditional boundaries, combining fashion, art, sports, and popular culture into wearable expressions of creativity and exclusivity. As the future unfolds, we can expect sneaker collaborations to continue captivating enthusiasts, breaking new ground, and shaping the landscape of fashion and footwear.

Sneaker Cleaning and Restoration Techniques

Sneakers have become an essential part of modern fashion, but keeping them clean and well-maintained can be a challenging task. Over time, sneakers accumulate dirt, stains, scuffs, and other imperfections that can detract from their overall appearance. However, with proper cleaning and restoration techniques, you can bring your sneakers back to their original glory. In this comprehensive guide, we will explore various methods and tips for sneaker cleaning and restoration.

Gathering the Necessary Tools:

Before delving into the cleaning process, it's crucial to assemble the right tools. Here are some essential items you'll need:

a. Soft-bristled brush: Ideal for removing loose dirt and debris from the sneaker's surface.

b. Microfiber cloth: Perfect for wiping off excess moisture and applying cleaning solutions.

c. Sneaker cleaning solution: Choose a mild and non-abrasive solution suitable for the shoe material.

d. Stain remover: For stubborn stains that require extra attention.

e. Sneaker protector spray: To create a protective barrier against future stains and damage.

f. Q-tips or cotton swabs: Useful for detailed cleaning of hard-to-reach areas.

g. Toothbrush: Excellent for cleaning midsoles and outsoles.

h. Suede brush or eraser: Specifically for cleaning and restoring suede sneakers.

i. Shoe trees or crumpled paper: Helps maintain the shoe's shape during the cleaning process.

Preparing the Sneakers:

Before starting the cleaning process, take the following preparatory steps:

a. Remove the shoelaces: Take off the laces to clean them separately or replace them if necessary.

b. Knock off excess dirt: Gently tap the sneakers together or use a soft brush to remove loose dirt and debris.

Cleaning Techniques:

a. General Sneaker Cleaning:

i. Spot cleaning: Dampen a microfiber cloth with the cleaning solution and gently rub the affected areas in circular motions.

ii. Deep cleaning: If the sneakers are heavily soiled, submerge them in a mixture of warm water and the cleaning solution. Use a soft brush to scrub the surface, paying attention to stains and scuffs. Rinse with clean water afterward.

iii. Midsole and outsole cleaning: Apply the cleaning solution to a toothbrush and scrub the midsole and outsole, focusing on textured areas to remove dirt and grime.

iv. Tongue and inner lining: Wipe the tongue and inner lining with a clean cloth dampened with the cleaning solution.

b. Suede Sneaker Cleaning:

i. Brushing: Use a suede brush or eraser to gently remove dirt and restore the suede's texture. Brush in one direction to prevent damage.

ii. Stain removal: For stubborn stains on suede, apply a small amount of suede cleaner or vinegar to a cloth and blot the stained area. Avoid excessive moisture.

iii. Reviving the nap: After cleaning, use a suede brush to restore the suede's nap by brushing it in multiple directions.

c. Leather Sneaker Cleaning:

i. Removing surface dirt: Wipe the sneakers with a damp cloth to remove surface dirt and dust.

ii. Cleaning and conditioning: Apply a small amount of leather cleaner to a cloth and gently clean the leather in circular motions. Once dry, apply a leather conditioner to restore moisture and prevent cracking.

Restoration Techniques:

a. Scuff and Scratch Removal:

i. Toothpaste method: Apply a small amount of toothpaste to a soft cloth and gently rub the scuffed area in circular motions. Wipe off the excess toothpaste and polish with a clean cloth.

ii. Nail polish remover: Dampen a cotton swab with nail polish remover and gently rub over the scuff or scratch. Wipe away any residue and apply a leather conditioner if necessary.

b. Dealing with Discoloration:

i. White vinegar: Mix equal parts of white vinegar and water, dampen a cloth with the solution, and gently wipe the discolored area. Rinse with clean water and pat dry.

ii. Bleach pen (for white sneakers): Use a bleach pen to carefully apply bleach to the discolored areas. Test it on a small, inconspicuous area first and follow the instructions.

c. Sole Regeneration:

i. Restoring yellowed soles: Mix a solution of equal parts water and hydrogen peroxide. Apply the mixture to the yellowed soles using a cloth or cotton ball. Leave it in direct sunlight for a few hours or use a UV light to accelerate the process. Rinse with water and let it air dry.

ii. Paint touch-up: If the soles have chips or scuffs, use a paint marker or acrylic paint to touch up the affected areas. Make sure to match the color as closely as possible.

Regular cleaning and proper maintenance can significantly prolong the lifespan of your sneakers and keep them looking fresh. By following the cleaning and restoration techniques outlined in this comprehensive guide, you can revive even the most worn-out sneakers. Remember to be gentle, use the appropriate tools and cleaning solutions for your shoe material, and always test any cleaning or restoration method on a small, inconspicuous area first. With patience and care, you'll be able to restore your sneakers to their former glory and enjoy them for years to come.

60 Super Popular And Hot Sneaker Brands For Resellers

Nike: Nike is a global leader in athletic footwear and apparel. Known for their innovative designs and iconic Air technology.

Adidas: Adidas is a renowned brand that offers a wide range of athletic footwear, with a focus on sportswear and lifestyle shoes.

Jordan Brand: A subsidiary of Nike, Jordan Brand specializes in basketball shoes inspired by legendary basketball player Michael Jordan.

Puma: Puma is a German multinational brand known for its sportswear, including sneakers that blend style and performance.

Converse: Converse is famous for its classic Chuck Taylor All Star sneakers, which have become a symbol of casual fashion.

Reebok: Reebok is a global athletic brand that offers a diverse range of sneakers, particularly known for their fitness and training shoes.

New Balance: New Balance is known for its comfortable and supportive sneakers, with a focus on performance and athletic footwear.

Vans: Vans is recognized for its skateboarding shoes, as well as casual and lifestyle sneakers that embody a laid-back California style.

ASICS: ASICS is a Japanese brand that specializes in performance running shoes, offering excellent cushioning and support for athletes.

Under Armour: Under Armour produces sneakers for various sports and activities, with a reputation for combining style and functionality.

Skechers: Skechers offers a wide range of sneakers for casual wear, athletics, and performance, known for their comfort and trendy designs.

Balenciaga: Balenciaga is a luxury fashion brand that has gained popularity for its chunky and exaggerated sneakers that make a bold fashion statement.

Yeezy: Yeezy is a collaboration between Adidas and musician Kanye West, featuring stylish and sought-after sneakers known for their limited availability.

Off-White: Off-White, led by designer Virgil Abloh, offers unique and fashion-forward sneakers that often incorporate deconstructed elements.

Gucci: Gucci, a renowned luxury brand, produces high-end sneakers with distinctive designs and premium materials.

Fila: Fila is an Italian sportswear brand that offers sneakers ranging from retro-inspired designs to modern athletic footwear.

Salomon: Salomon is known for its performance sneakers designed for outdoor activities such as trail running and hiking.

Balmain: Balmain is a luxury fashion brand that creates stylish and elegant sneakers, often featuring intricate details and premium craftsmanship.

Maison Margiela: Maison Margiela is a high-end fashion house that produces avant-garde sneakers characterized by their deconstructed and unconventional designs.

Asics Tiger: Asics Tiger is a lifestyle division of ASICS that combines retro aesthetics with modern comfort, offering sneakers inspired by their heritage.

Brooks: Brooks specializes in running shoes, providing a wide range of sneakers for different running styles and preferences.

Hoka One One: Hoka One One is known for its maximalist running shoes, offering excellent cushioning and support for long-distance runners.

Vans Vault: Vans Vault is a premium line from Vans that

showcases collaborations and limited-edition sneakers with unique materials and designs.

Diadora: Diadora is an Italian brand that produces athletic footwear, including sneakers for various sports, with a focus on heritage-inspired designs.

Etnies: Etnies is a skateboarding footwear brand known for its durable and skate-ready sneakers, favored by professional skateboarders.

Timberland: Timberland is famous for its rugged and durable boots but also offers a range of sneakers that blend outdoor functionality with urban style.

Onitsuka Tiger: Onitsuka Tiger is a Japanese brand that specializes in retro-style sneakers, featuring classic designs inspired by the brand's heritage.

Saucony: Saucony is a popular brand for runners, known for its performance-oriented running shoes that offer a balance of cushioning and responsiveness.

Vionic: Vionic focuses on comfort and foot health, offering sneakers with supportive features and advanced orthopedic technology.

Fendi: Fendi is a luxury fashion brand that creates high-end sneakers, often featuring the brand's signature logo and luxurious materials.

Versace: Versace is a luxury fashion brand that offers high-end sneakers with bold designs, often incorporating the brand's iconic Medusa logo.

Burberry: Burberry is known for its British heritage and offers stylish sneakers featuring the brand's distinctive check pattern and premium materials.

Balenciaga Track: Balenciaga Track sneakers are known for their chunky, multi-layered design and have gained popularity for their fashion-forward and futuristic aesthetic.

Givenchy: Givenchy is a luxury fashion brand that produces sleek and stylish sneakers, often incorporating unique details and premium craftsmanship.

Alexander McQueen: Alexander McQueen sneakers are known for their edgy and avant-garde designs, often featuring exaggerated soles and intricate detailing.

Acne Studios: Acne Studios offers minimalist and contemporary sneakers, characterized by clean lines, understated designs, and premium materials.

Common Projects: Common Projects focuses on minimalist sneakers with clean silhouettes and subtle branding, known for their high-quality construction and luxury aesthetic.

Lanvin: Lanvin is a luxury fashion brand that produces elegant and sophisticated sneakers, combining refined craftsmanship with modern design elements.

Rick Owens: Rick Owens is known for his avant-garde and unconventional sneaker designs, often featuring unique silhouettes and experimental materials.

Maison Kitsuné: Maison Kitsuné offers sneakers with a blend of streetwear and high fashion aesthetics, featuring playful designs and premium craftsmanship.

Kenzo: Kenzo is a luxury brand that creates vibrant and eclectic sneakers, often incorporating bold prints, colors, and unique textures.

Saint Laurent: Saint Laurent is renowned for its luxurious and rock-inspired sneakers, featuring sleek designs, premium materials, and iconic branding.

Lanvin: Lanvin is a French fashion house known for its sophisticated and refined sneakers, often featuring elegant detailing and premium craftsmanship.

Filling Pieces: Filling Pieces offers contemporary sneakers with a focus on craftsmanship and unique design elements, blending streetwear aesthetics with luxury materials.

Visvim: Visvim is a Japanese brand that produces high-quality sneakers influenced by traditional craftsmanship and featuring unique details and materials.

Asics Gel-Lyte: Asics Gel-Lyte sneakers are known for their retro-inspired designs and comfortable cushioning, combining nostalgia with modern performance features.

Karhu: Karhu is a Finnish brand that specializes in running shoes, known for their innovative technologies and distinctive designs inspired by Finnish nature and culture.

Diemme: Diemme is an Italian brand that produces premium sneakers with a focus on high-quality materials, craftsmanship, and functional design.

Clarks: Clarks is a British brand known for its classic and timeless sneakers, particularly famous for its iconic desert boots and Wallabees.

Novesta: Novesta is a Slovakian brand that offers sustainable sneakers made from natural materials, known for their minimalist designs and chunky soles.

Veja: Veja is a sustainable sneaker brand that prioritizes ethical production and eco-friendly materials, offering stylish and eco-conscious footwear options.

Ecco: Ecco is a Danish brand that combines comfort and functionality in its sneakers, known for their innovative technologies and premium craftsmanship.

Camper: Camper is a Spanish brand that produces contemporary sneakers with a focus on comfort and unique design elements, offering a balance of style and functionality.

On Running: On Running specializes in performance running shoes, offering sneakers with responsive cushioning and innovative technologies for enhanced running experiences.

Mizuno: Mizuno is a Japanese brand that produces high-performance running shoes, known for their advanced technologies and precise engineering for optimal performance.

K-Swiss: K-Swiss is an American brand that offers classic and retro-inspired sneakers, particularly known for their iconic tennis shoes and clean designs.

Supra: Supra is a skateboarding footwear brand that

produces sneakers with bold designs and skate-ready features, favored by professional skateboarders and urban fashion enthusiasts.

Swear: Swear is a London-based brand that offers customizable sneakers, allowing customers to choose various materials, colors, and design details to create their own unique pair.

Columbia: Columbia is a brand specializing in outdoor footwear, including sneakers designed for hiking and trail running, with features such as waterproofing and traction.

Hi-Tec: Hi-Tec is known for its affordable and durable sneakers designed for outdoor activities such as hiking, walking, and casual adventures, providing comfort and functionality.

10 Sneaker Trade Shows That Sneaker Resellers Will Love

Sneaker Con: One of the largest sneaker events globally, Sneaker Con features exhibitions, vendor booths, and trading opportunities for sneaker enthusiasts.

ComplexCon: ComplexCon combines music, art, fashion, and sneakers, attracting a diverse audience. It includes exclusive product drops, panel discussions, and live performances.

The Sole DXB: Held in Dubai, The Sole DXB showcases sneakers, streetwear, and urban culture. It features brand activations, panel talks, and performances from local and international artists.

Agenda Trade Show: A leading trade show for lifestyle, streetwear, and action sports, Agenda includes sneaker brands alongside other fashion and lifestyle exhibitors.

Sneakerness: Originating in Europe and expanding globally, Sneakerness brings together sneaker enthusiasts, retailers, and collectors. It offers a marketplace for buying, selling, and trading sneakers.

Sneaker Summit: Established in Houston, Sneaker Summit has become a prominent gathering for sneakerheads and includes vendor booths, sneaker showcases, and special collaborations.

Solemart: Organized in Berlin, Solemart is a European sneaker convention that provides a platform for buying, selling, and trading sneakers, as well as networking with industry professionals.

Sneaker Pimps: Started as a sneaker art exhibition, Sneaker Pimps evolved into a worldwide tour featuring sneaker showcases, musical performances, and art installations.

Sneaker Exchange: Based in South Africa, Sneaker

Exchange brings together local sneaker enthusiasts and offers a platform for buying, selling, and trading sneakers, as well as showcasing local streetwear brands.

Kicks on Fire: Kicks on Fire is an annual sneaker event held in Chicago, featuring vendor booths, panel discussions, and live entertainment. It focuses on sneaker culture, fashion, and industry insights.

Ready To Manufacture Your Own Sneaker Line? These 10 Sneaker Factories Are Ready To Make Your Dreams Come True!

Yue Yuen Industrial Holdings Limited: Yue Yuen is one of the largest athletic shoe manufacturers in the world, with factories in China. They produce footwear for renowned brands like Nike, Adidas, Puma, and others.

Dongguan Gaobu Sports Shoe Factory: Located in Dongguan, Guangdong Province, this factory specializes in the production of sports shoes and sneakers. It works with various international brands and has a significant manufacturing capacity.

Huajian Group: Huajian is a prominent footwear manufacturer based in Dongguan, Guangdong Province. While they produce a wide range of shoes, they also manufacture sneakers for global brands.

Anta Sports: Anta Sports is a leading sportswear company in China. They operate their own production facilities and manufacture sneakers under their brand name, as well as for other partners.

Peak Sport Products Co., Ltd: Peak Sport is another major Chinese sportswear brand that produces sneakers and other athletic footwear. They have factories in various locations in China, including Quanzhou.

Xtep International Holdings Limited: Xtep is a Chinese footwear company specializing in sports shoes. They have multiple manufacturing facilities across China and cater to both domestic and international markets.

Feng Tay Enterprises: Feng Tay is an established footwear manufacturer based in Taiwan, with factories in China. They work with renowned brands to produce a range of shoes, including sneakers.

Belle International Holdings Limited: Belle International is one of the largest shoe retailers in China, and they also have their own manufacturing facilities. They produce a variety of footwear, including sneakers, under their own brand and for other companies.

Fujian Putian Best Co., Ltd: Based in Putian, Fujian Province, this factory focuses on the production of replica sneakers. They manufacture sneakers that closely resemble popular brands, but please note that replica products may infringe on intellectual property rights.

Jinjiang Footwear Industry Association: Jinjiang, located in Fujian Province, is a renowned hub for sneaker manufacturing. The region is home to numerous footwear factories, and the Jinjiang Footwear Industry Association can provide information on multiple factories operating in the area.

Conclusion:

"The Art of Reselling Sneakers" has taken us on a captivating journey into the world of sneaker reselling, illuminating the passion, strategy, and relentless pursuit of success that define this vibrant industry. Through the pages of this book, we have explored the evolving landscape of sneaker culture, delved into the intricate economics of limited edition releases, and unraveled the secrets of successful resellers who have turned their love for sneakers into thriving businesses.

Throughout our exploration, one prevailing theme emerges: reselling sneakers is far more than just a means of making a profit. It is a testament to the human desire for connection, self-expression, and the thrill of the chase. Sneakerheads and resellers alike demonstrate an unwavering commitment to their craft, spending countless hours researching, networking, and staying one step ahead of the ever-changing trends and market demands.

We have witnessed the power of authenticity and brand loyalty, where the value of a sneaker extends far beyond its material worth. Sneakers become symbols of personal identity, cultural significance, and artistic expression. Resellers play a vital role in ensuring that coveted releases reach the hands of those who truly appreciate and cherish them.

Yet, as the industry continues to grow, challenges and ethical considerations come to the fore. The battle against counterfeit sneakers, the impact on the environment, and the concerns of accessibility and inclusivity are all topics that demand our attention and collective efforts. "Sole Pursuit" encourages us to reflect on the responsible and sustainable practices we can adopt to preserve the integrity and future of sneaker reselling.

Ultimately, this book serves as both a comprehensive guide and a source of inspiration for aspiring resellers, sneaker enthusiasts, and anyone curious about the dynamic world that exists at the intersection of fashion, culture, and entrepreneurship. It celebrates the entrepreneurial spirit, resourcefulness, and dedication of individuals who have turned their passion into a viable business, while reminding us of the profound impact sneakers can have on our lives.

As we conclude this journey, one thing becomes clear: the art of reselling sneakers is an ever-evolving endeavor that requires adaptability, tenacity, and a genuine love for the craft. May this book inspire readers to embrace their own passions, chase their dreams, and leave an indelible mark on the world—one sneaker at a time.

www.ingramcontent.com/pod-product-compliance
Lightning Source LLC
Chambersburg PA
CBHW070426240526
45472CB00020B/1460